Little Science Stories

Did It Grow?

By Amanda Gebhardt

 Plants help us grow big. You can help plants grow big.

What helps plants grow?
Set up this test.

4   Set four cups. Fill them up.

Press a spot in.

 Set a seed in each spot.

Fill each spot.

Set two cups in the sun.
Set two cups in the shade.

Add water to one cup
in the sun.

Add water to one cup
in the shade.

Mark each cup you watered.

Water those cups each day.
Wait and see. Look each day.

Which plants grew? What did
they need?

Word List

science words

grow	seed
grew	sun
need	test
Plants	water
plants	watered

sight words

a	two
four	water
Mark	Water
one	watered
the	What
to	

Vowel Teams

/ā/ai, ay, ey	/ē/ea, ee	/ō/ow	/o͞o/ew, ou	/o͝o/oo
day	each	grow	grew	Look
they	need		You	
Wait	see		you	
	seed			

14

Try It!
See how plants grow! Follow the steps in the book.
Write what happens. Tell what plants need to grow.

89 Words

Plants help us grow big. You can help plants grow big.

What helps plants grow? Set up this test.

Set four cups. Fill them up.

Press a spot in.

Set a seed in each spot.

Fill each spot.

Set two cups in the sun. Set two cups in the shade.

Add water to one cup in the sun.

Add water to one cup in the shade.

Mark each cup you watered.

Water those cups each day. Wait and see. Look each day.

Which plants grew? What did they need?

CHERRY BLOSSOM PRESS

Published in the United States of America by Cherry Lake Publishing Group
Ann Arbor, Michigan
www.cherrylakepublishing.com

Photo Credits: © PEACE ECOLOGY/Shutterstock, cover, title page; © Ana Blazic Pavlovic/ Shutterstock, 2; © Pinkyone/Shutterstock, 3; © David Moreno Hernandez/Dreamstime.com, 4; © David Moreno Hernandez/Dreamstime.com, 5; © Svett/Shutterstock, 6; © David Moreno Hernandez/Dreamstime.com, 7; © Viktor Sergeevich/Shutterstock, 8; © New Africa/Shutterstock, 9; © Belavusava Alena/Shutterstock, 10; © Chernetskaya/Dreamstime.com, 11; © encierro/ Shutterstock, 12; © David Tadevosian/Shutterstock, 13; © Stanisl Av/Shutterstock, back cover

Cherry Blossom Press is an imprint of Cherry Lake Publishing Group.

Library of Congress Cataloging-in-Publication Data

Names: Gebhardt, Amanda, author.
Title: Did it grow? / written by Amanda Gebhardt.
Description: Ann Arbor, Michigan : Cherry Blossom Press, [2024] | Series: Little science stories | Audience: Grades K-1 | Summary: "Learn what plants need to grow in this decodable science book for beginning readers. A combination of domain-specific sight words and sequenced phonics skills builds confidence in content area reading. Bold, colorful photographs align directly with the text to help readers strengthen comprehension"– Provided by publisher.
Identifiers: LCCN 2023035052 | ISBN 9781668937648 (paperback) | ISBN 9781668940020 (ebook) | ISBN 9781668941379 (pdf)
Subjects: LCSH: Growth (Plants)–Juvenile literature. | Plants–Development–Juvenile literature. | Plants–Effect of light on–Juvenile literature. | Plants–Effect of water levels on–Juvenile literature.
Classification: LCC QK731 .G43 2024 | DDC 581–dc23/eng/20230831
LC record available at https://lccn.loc.gov/2023035052

Printed in the United States of America

Amanda Gebhardt is a curriculum writer and editor and a life-long learner. She lives in Ann Arbor, Michigan, with her husband, two kids, and one playful pup named Cookie.